DIGITAL CLASSROOM

AN IDEA THAT GIVES MEANING TO MY LIFE.

ASHISH MALHOTRA

Copyright © Ashish Malhotra
All Rights Reserved.

This book has been self-published with all reasonable efforts taken to make the material error-free by the author. No part of this book shall be used, reproduced in any manner whatsoever without written permission from the author, except in the case of brief quotations embodied in critical articles and reviews.

The Author of this book is solely responsible and liable for its content including but not limited to the views, representations, descriptions, statements, information, opinions and references ["Content"]. The Content of this book shall not constitute or be construed or deemed to reflect the opinion or expression of the Publisher or Editor. Neither the Publisher nor Editor endorse or approve the Content of this book or guarantee the reliability, accuracy or completeness of the Content published herein and do not make any representations or warranties of any kind, express or implied, including but not limited to the implied warranties of merchantability, fitness for a particular purpose. The Publisher and Editor shall not be liable whatsoever for any errors, omissions, whether such errors or omissions result from negligence, accident, or any other cause or claims for loss or damages of any kind, including without limitation, indirect or consequential loss or damage arising out of use, inability to use, or about the reliability, accuracy or sufficiency of the information contained in this book.

Made with ♥ on the Notion Press Platform
www.notionpress.com

To my parents, Sh. Brij Bhushan Malhotra and Smt. Neerja.

Contents

Mr. Ashish Malhotra was born to an artist mother and a social leader and public figure father in a small town Dhariwal, near Amritsar in Punjab, India. His father is running a grocery store in the town. His mother is a housewife. She was a very good painter. She dropped her painting career after her marriage. His father was a social worker and therefore, was very much involved in the local politics. His father has worked for forty years for the society. His father has faced a lot of ups and downs in his life. Ashish had witnessed a lot of critical situations in his father's life. His father has earned a lot of respect in the society. Ashish also wanted to do something for the society. From childhood, he was very sensitive toward society issues. So, he decided to spread awareness in the students about "Ideals and Morals". That was the start of his new journey. Since then he started taking more interest in philosophy and worked as a philosophy professor in a college and later wrote and self-published his first book "How I reached my passion".

He studied Aircraft Maintenance engineering from Delhi and then worked for five years in the aviation sector and later decided to leave his job for the social cause.

He has also studied Modern applied psychology and now he is pursuing BA in psychology from Vivekananda global university, Jaipur and also instructor at Udemy and published his own course at Udemy. You can find the details of his course at www.udemy.com/course/selfempowerment and www.udemy.com/course/Aimhigh-Dreamhigh

He is also rewarded by "Gandhi smriti and Darshan samiti, autonomous body of ministry of culture,

Government of India" for his social work "ideals and Morals" in the year 2020 under the contest name "story on karyanjali". More details available at mygov.in.

Hope you all will like his dedication and writing.

The days in Kailash were beautiful days and I was missing my new family at Kailash. I was missing my mother Parvati and two brothers with whom I enjoy the lessons and the food which mother had prepared for us with so much fondness. Renunciation had done its work and now it is the time to share what I had learned and gained from my mentor Shiva. So, I returned back to the city Bangalore to start my mission of uplifting students about the knowledge which we all were lacking. But I did not understand where I should start?

I had no idea of the responsibility which had been given to me by my mentor. I had no money, no accommodation but I had few friends and a beautiful family which maintains a paying guest in Bangalore which I had left before the meeting.

They were the only hope. So, I went to them. I told them about the meeting and they were surprised and told me "I am lying to them". "It is impossible".

"How could anyone meet Shiva?", they asked.

This was the question which had taken me aback. How can I explain to them the meeting?

I tell them the truth to meet Shiva or I should make up the story?

Better I should tell them the truth.

I told the mother who was the caretaker of the paying guest, I am feeling hungry so please give me some food first. She served me the food. I enjoyed the food. Mother was looking at me astonishingly as I was licking my fingers. She was happy when I told her, "the food was so delicious".

On one condition I will tell you the story if you will serve me the delicious food day and night, I told her.

She agreed and smiled.

Ok, then we will meet tomorrow as I had to visit some schools and I had to prepare for that.

She had provided me with the food and the room. I told her whenever I had the money I would pay her.

She smiled in the reaction and said, do not worry about the money and stay as long as you want.

Namaste, I said and left for the room.

She was living with her husband on the ground floor and had a son and a daughter in law and two grandsons living along. She was blessed with a happy and honest son and hard working daughter in law. Her son was working as a delivery agent in some ekart services and her daughter-in-law maintains the house chores. Her daughter-in-law also helped her in making the chapaati's as she did not know how to cook the chapaati's. I sometimes helped her grandsons by providing tuitions after their school in the evening. It was the same love and respect given to me as I had experienced in Kailash by the whole family. I was thankful to the Shiva who had told me to lead the way and experience love and pain in the journey.

1

The journey

Next morning, I bathed and became ready to visit some schools. I did not know where I should start the journey? Doubts were popping up in my head. Could I complete the mission? Without giving much thought I had taken out the diary and started writing down the school's name. I found so many schools in the vicinity and I called them one by one. There was not a single satisfied response from the other side of the call.

I decided to go to the schools and talk to them personally. This is the best action right now for you to start the journey, I told myself.

So, I dressed up and hired a yulu bicycle service. I decided to cover schools one by one in each area. I decided to first cover the area near which I was living. There were some schools and I went to each and every school.

After noon, I returned home tired and mother told me to eat lunch on time. I told her, I will eat the dinner as I promised to myself to not eat much until I will not attain the results.

"But why are you acting so hard on yourself?" she asked me.

"I am not acting hard", I replied with a smile. I was practicing the discipline. Otherwise these comforts would take me toward laziness and I would not take up the responsibility.

She smiled and agreed with the notion. I knew that she was eagerly waiting for the answer of her question which she asked me last day. But I ignored her curiosity and left for the room.

It was not easy to convince school principals about the mission. I was tired because of riding the bicycle after so many years. My thighs were in pain. I was craving hunger but I couldn't eat as I had decided to maintain discipline. But I was satisfied that I had acted. First day was good so far. I went back to the room and rested a little bit before going to the park.

Later that evening I met the mother and decided to give her the answer to her question. I told her that the first thing we needed to do if we wanted to meet Shiva was to have a mission. The mission which showcases your vision, your aim. It may be your personal motive or it may include the whole society or the country or the world. That was the first condition.

My mission was based on the rising social problem of youth becoming dependent upon jobs and losing their vision which was in the long term affecting their potential. Mentally, our youth was lacking a vision and the power to become self-dependent. The major problem with most of them was that they were not aware about the consequences of this. They would not only lose their independence but also their value. Value is the product of our aim.

Also, that lack of self-dependency contributes toward our irresponsible behavior. That irresponsible behavior further affects the work culture, the social culture and the spoilage of our parenthood and the major effect of this irresponsible behavior is it has emaciated us.

So, therefore, I had decided to help the adolescents. I will make them aware about their internal strength and the power of their potential.

Mother was surprised by the words which were coming out of my mouth. She was not aware of my motive and also, she was taking it as a union which liberated me, freed me from my duties and I now become a monk. Most of us think it was in the way as it had been shown to us through so many mythological dramas.

People had not the slightest idea that to meet the beloved we had to be responsible toward our-self first. We had to confront our potential. Because our potential is the closest ally of the beloved.

Meeting Shiva, as I said it before, needs the mission which is centered around the goal. Social responsibility comes to those who had the vision to find out the solutions. One can only solve social problems when he has the ability to solve them. Ability comes to those who have the goal. Therefore, it is our supreme duty to make our goal and find out our potential so that we can meet Shiva and also use that potential to contribute toward the society.

"We all had been fooled by the society around us all these years who gave us this thought that to meet your beloved you had to wait for old age or you had to renounce everything if you want to meet him or this all depends upon luck.

This social ignorance and their beliefs not only harm the career of the adolescents but also the integrity of the society and the country. This belief had made a child mentally weaker and distanced him from the closest ally of the beloved that is his potential.

Potential is the only weapon which can unite us with the infinite power which is not residing anywhere in the outer world but in our inner world, in the depth of our mind."

Mother was awestruck with the intensity of the words.

Then after a silence of two minutes she asked me, "how will you do this?"

I had to follow a process.

A process! What do you mean?

Be patient, said I. I had my dinner. Food was amazingly delicious. Then I went to my room and slept while planning for the next day.

2

A Vision

One thing was clear to me that my target is adolescents. Best way to meet them are the schools. To carry on my mission, I had to consistently keep visiting the schools. But I did not know how these schools would react to my vision.

Would they allow me or reject me? Rather giving it a second thought, I bathed and dressed up for the journey. I had my breakfast and left.

My vision was clear to me. I had to convince the principal about the mission.

After spending four hours on the journey I came back at noon. I had bought the curd sachet for ten and drank it. Mother asked me how was the day? Journey was tiring, said I. But it gives me pleasure.

Had any principal convinced? asked mother.

No.

Then how did you feel pleasure?

The journey was tiring but what if I say the process is the journey!

What do you mean? asked mother.

The things looked at the outer realm very harsh but in the internal realm it is the constructive progress. It constructs your psychology. It shapes the vision.

I start with a vision consisting of an idea which carries in itself the energy of the divine. This energy not only makes the journey but it constructs you internally in a very scientific way.

For example, it shapes your vision. As you keep working on your idea it will shape your idea into a reality. How?

Because of the divine energy which is present in every life, constructing it like a small sapling grows gradually into a plant having potential to create medicine or so many things.

How does this small sapling contain the potential? Where does it come from?

This is the science which works in the background of every life. It depends on life which way it wants to use science.

Our environment is the medium in which life survives. If our environment consists of toxicity, hate and meaning less aims it will activate the destructive phase of science in life.

For example, if there are two sons of a mother and the mother puts these two sons into two different environments. One into the company of a great teacher, which teaches him the beliefs which make him an honest and hardworking and a person who loves humanity and to the other, into the company of a leader which taught him to take revenge, make him a hateful and angry person toward some other group. In both cases, if we carefully look, one aims for the good of the other and one aims for the bad of the other. How? The environment plays a major role.

The beliefs created by those two mentors went deep into the depth of the mind. There they sow like a seed. The mentor had created the environment and nourished those seeds and later with the age, they took their shape which was hard enough for anyone to reshape it again.

Now if you give the child the belief to create a valuable goal in his life and blend it with a noble character he will definitely raise in the environment of his own constructive science which works in the background away from everyone's sight. This constructive nature of the science is very harsh on the outer side because of its need. The need of constructive science are the beliefs which nourish him to a man of a valuable person.

The need for constructive science centered around the mind and the body of the child and any other person. Discipline is a very important element of constructive science which it uses as a tool by creating hard circumstances.

If you want to grow you have to be ready to face the heat of the sun and the aggression of the wind.

There is no other way to become capable and valuable and constructive at the inner side.

Understand it as you are constructing a home and you have to choose the elements to use as a concrete to fill the pillars and cement the wall of the home. If the concrete had not high compressive strength and not high alkaline in nature it will rust the iron and if the concrete had high compressive strength and high alkaline nature it will prevent it from the rust and it will stand strong and supportive.

Every belief which you give to your child sows there in the depth of his mind. So, it is a duty of the parents and the society and the teacher when you are acting near the child or teaching him, it must carry the message of love and the power of having a valuable goal. These actions and teachings will sow in the depth of his mind and take a shape there and it all depends on the nourishment which he is getting from his environment i.e. his parents, society and teachers. Nourishment is very important if we want to grow a healthy child. You can understand it very easily with the example of organic manure and inorganic manure. Organic nourishment takes much time to grow a crop but it grows them healthy. The same way when we nourish the child with the beliefs of love and a vision he will definitely grow a more valuable, more courageous and more intelligent person and it takes a more time to create his value than others because it uses the organic process.

That is the major difference between constructive science and destructive science.

Best advice which I get from Shiva is to change our-self. When we focus on our created beliefs then we understand how to grow as a person and become valuable in the society.

Therefore, it is very important to understand if as a person anyone wants to grow he must have to set a high aim which sows in the depth of his mind and gradually takes the shape there and make him a visionary person, a person of caliber.

There are so many people in our society who create the wrong beliefs which further destroy them internally.

For example, people commonly say, "I am getting what is written in my destiny".

But are they sure that" had they explored every aspect of their destiny which will open them some new way of their destiny?" "Had they tried all the possible actions to discover their potential?" "Had they explored the scope of their potential?"

Most probably you will get the "no" in their answer.

Most of the time, people act lazy and what they do is to depend on others or wait for someone to come and rescue them from their problems or expect too much from their government, keep complaining about the government and their established systems. The surprising thing is that they are the same people who are abusing the government, working in their system, exploiting their resources and the people.

They built the habit of dependence on the jobs. Why? Because they had been taught from their childhood to secure your future and the easiest way to do that is to get the job.

They had been filled with the fear of life.

The saddest part is most of the adults in our society are lacking vision and the potential to create something. They are lacking courage to take the risks and to enjoy the journey called life. They have been busy wasting their time securing life which is like holding sand tightly in their hands.

They do not know that life is a phenomenon which works on science. As I described before, everything is working on science. Science is the essence of every life. It constructs you or destructs you depending on your vision about life and the belief sowed into the depth of your mind.

So, it is very important for everybody to understand that science is the language of the gods. If you want to talk to god, if you want to meet the god you have to understand this language i.e. science.

The best way to understand science is to not understand science. But to focus on two things: one is to set a vision and second is to build the character. There is a great power residing in having a vision and a noble character. They will link you to the infinite wisdom and power which is residing nowhere but in the depths of your mind. You do not know how to look into that and therefore you are wasting all your life wasting it to secure your outer circumstances rather than giving meaning to life.

Therefore, learn to look into the depth of your mind and reconstruct your beliefs for the betterment of your life.

So, you mean to say that to meet Shiva we had to build a vision and a strong character? asked mother.

Absolutely. Without these two fundamental necessities of each and every life no one can meet Shiva.

The necessities are very simple. Just to set an aim and work on them. As I said, the environment is nourishing. So, parents, home culture, society, friends and teachers will give that environment to the child to grow him as a valuable person.

Remember that construction will take time. This is the law. When we are building something, give it time. Otherwise it will not learn the lessons which the journey had for him which is important for him to grow and become the best version of himself.

I left the mother alone with their thoughts and came back to my room. She was now definitely having the idea of the meeting.

3

Patriotism

I had tried so many schools in the past month and finally, I got one school to volunteer. I love the locality of the school. It took me three hours from my place to reach the village where the school is located. School had such a mesmerizing classroom in the shape of the pyramids. When I entered the place, I felt so proud of my efforts and the process which took me so far to the beautiful school.

"Journey is not only providing you the opportunity to meet like minded people but also gives you so much pleasure and satisfaction at the psychological level. It had its own way to give you the richness. As Buddha once said, every cause had an effect."

I met the representative of the school and he was a little more than my father. I told him the reason for coming there and the motive behind the volunteering. He was such a gentleman. He was so quick with his answers and proud of his efforts of building the school. He told me that he and his family maintained this school. The reason to run the school in the village is to provide the education to the nearby children of the villages. He said, I want every child to be educated irrespective of his background and financial status. That's the reason I opened this school with my sisters and now it has more than two hundred and fifty students.

He told me to start your session immediately. I do not want you to waste your such a long journey from the city to the countryside and therefore, please proceed to the classroom.

It was such a proud moment for me as to what responsibility had been given to me by my mentor. I had finally delivered my vision to the adolescents which I carried with me from last one month. Finally, I felt that I had contributed to the betterment of society. These adolescents will someday become a responsible citizen in the form of an engineer, athlete, doctor, an industrialist and artist and help in their country's potential to grow and make it a better place. A place where everyone is respecting each other's talent and helping each other to grow.

I came back to my room. Money was the issue. As one month had passed and I had to pay the mother a room rent. I decided to tutor the students to gain some income. So, I started exploring the tutoring application on my mobile phone and registered myself in one of the apps. Soon, in a period of two days I got my first student to tutor. I went to her place after volunteering. She was very young, almost in the sixth standard and I had to tutor her on every subject. She was very adorable and was very adjustable otherwise it became very tough to tutor the teen for me.

Days were passing like springtime. So beautiful and so much of abundance. I was enjoying this new journey as I had no idea a few months back how this journey would take shape?

The only thing which I required now was more and more students and therefore, I started meeting more and more principals.

I had paid my rent in a month's gap. Mother was happy with the progression. But she looks sad therefore I went to her to ask her about the matter. She said, I now have a better understanding than before. Now I felt that I had wasted my life. Because I never had created any goal in my life. As her mother always told her to learn the house chores and therefore, she never went to school to study.

I told her that education is the most important tool if we want to meet Shiva. But what is education? What is the meaning of educating our-self?

Most of the adolescents are studying with a motive to get a job or the money or to marry and to start a family or because their parents had promised them to buy them a car or a smartphone etc. if they will get the good percentage. These are the motives of most of the adolescents that are studying.

Their motive is not learning but to achieve success and enjoy the comforts and that creates the consequences in their life. Consequences are the results of our motive.

How will they understand the meaning of education with these motives? And what will they contribute with these motives into the society?

And the question here arises: who had created these motives in the child about education? And with these kinds of motives how can you become successful?

Education is the years we spend on learning. Education is not measured by the qualification you had but how much you had learnt?

Have you learned anything in your life? Have you learned to use your knowledge?

These are the simple questions we need to ask our- self. Learning is the essence of the education system, otherwise what is the meaning of educating our-self. We must give much focus on learning the skills. See the whole market is filled with the skilled people that are running the businesses there. But in our education system there is not a single skill we are sharing with the students. There are photographers, tailors, chefs, merchants, designers, electrician, plumber, mechanic, doctor, pharmacist and so on.

But in our education system we are teaching them to get good marks. How will they be a good learner? When our education system and parents and society all three main pillars of the development of the child are focusing on getting good marks rather than to be a great learner.

But the real victims are the girls like you. They had no idea about the power of education because they had been busy with in-house chores and then they got married.

We are using education to grow externally not internally and that's the reason we are distancing our-self from Shiva. We need to understand that education is the medium to connect internally and disconnect externally. When we start to use the education to grow internally then we become the part of his realm where we will connect to him and his wisdom. There are scientists, engineers, doctors, athletes, artists and so many intelligent people in this world.

From where they are getting the power to think? From where they are getting the knowledge to create? From where they are getting the power to win?

Do you think a man had the power to create and destroy?

The man is the center of all the creation and destruction. But who is creating and destroying everything with time? That we need to ask our-self.

The energy which had created everything had first created the motive in the depth of the man's mind. Then it gives the desire to fulfill that motive and the courage to act on that motive.

Do you think a man can create desires?

No.

We all are controlled by our desires. These desires give us the roles, the character to play.

From where our thoughts are popping out?

In the depth of the mind there are so many desires, beliefs, fear, pleasures, anxiety, goals, hate, jealousy, ego which creates these thoughts on whom we react with our perception.

What do you think we are?

A nobody. We are completely under the control of this vastness. We had no idea that we were under their control. And the major element which creates the veil in truth and reality is the ego of the man.

The only way to reach the truth is through learning. Learn to give others. Learn to share with others. When you share with others it will make you humble and that humbleness is anti-ego. That will make you closer to your internal king.

The most important thing a man can share with the world is his potential. Therefore, it is the priority of every human being, be it a girl or a boy, that they must find out what kind of potential they are gifted with?

And you had not yet missed the chance, mother. You too can find your potential. You cook so well. Why don't you share these skills with others?

I left the mother with this question as I had to wake up early to catch the bus to reach the village on time.

But I am sure she definitely gets the importance of the idea of learning and sharing.

Parents, schools and society can change the meaning of education and therefore, it is everyone's responsibility to play the part to bring change in the definition of education. With these thoughts I slept for the role which I had to play the very next morning.

We use information most of the time when we are giving some exams. Because most of us had experienced that what we had learned in our school and colleges will forget with time.

This is the major difference with the information and knowledge. Information never remains with you and on the other hand, Knowledge always stays with you.

Information gives you the idea about the product. But if you want to gain the insights of how things work then you have to work on gaining knowledge which means to learn to explore your potential. In this way you can unite with nature from where every idea springs out.

The only quest you have is to find out your own potential.

Why is it important?

Because we all are made up of nature. Nature is the major element which constitutes every being on this planet, being it a human, insects, trees, animals, bacteria, other organisms etc.

The beautiful thing of nature has given us all some speciality. Like, a wood to become a matchstick, a paper, a tree to give oxygen and a land to grow the crop and to hide in its depth the oil and so many other qualities etc.

The same way a human being has been designated with so many specialties which he has to discover in this quest called life. That's the reason which gives meaning to our life.

Otherwise, why has this play been created?"

I had to find out the students in my hometown because this is really important for me that I should consistently work on my mission. Therefore, I started again visiting the schools in my hometown with the same intensity as before.

I had to reach more and more students. I soon got more than two schools to volunteer there. I had completed my sessions successfully in all the schools.

But this process was really tiring for me. Because I had to visit so many schools and convince them about the idea on which most of them showed no interest.

I felt like something was going wrong. Then once a famous college in my hometown had called me to teach there for three months because their philosophy lecturer had been hospitalized for some reason.

At first this opportunity made me happy but there was a tint of fear as I had never studied academic philosophy before. How would I teach the students?

But I was confident that I could handle it. So, I took up the opportunity. That opportunity has given me the platform to explore your potential. I took full advantage of that opportunity. The students started liking my teaching and they started enjoying my lectures. I also felt so much attachment with that place with the time.

This duty of mine was giving me so much pleasure, freedom and satisfaction at the psychological level.

That day I realized that at a psychological level every human being had only one need and that is to realize their potential.

We always focused on fulfilling our physical needs, be it food, shelter, money, sex, clothes. But what about the psychological need?

Parents and society and most of us are looking at the wrong side for happiness by fulfilling our physical needs. But what about the psychological needs? Real happiness drives from satisfaction at the psychological level.

How would they know that?

4
Hunger for Achievement

I had completed the sessions at my very first school and now I become more eager to reach more and more students and therefore, I started visiting more schools. I visited schools again and again. For months I had been rejected by so many schools. Some principals even disbelieve my motive and I felt tired. I did not realize once that it was so hard to make them believe in the sanctity of volunteering.

The idea which only wants to achieve their mission.

It reminds me of the representative of the school to whom I had met for the first time during the volunteering. He was so simple and a naive man. Without once thinking about the negative aspect of volunteering he was quick with his answer that if you want to help them then why will I stop you? It is our collective duty to help them make a better human being.

It was really hard to find a man like him. Finally, after one month I met a principal who really liked the idea of volunteering and told me to start your sessions from tomorrow. Thereafter, I met two or more principals who gave me the permission to run the sessions in their school and college.

I had covered almost five hundred students and then I went to volunteer at one more school before moving back to my hometown.

That school was far from my place and money was always an issue with me those days. I had to manage everything within the small income which I had from the tuition and the provident fund and also my friends help me with a small amount from their income and their pocket money. When I told them about my mission, some of them told me not to worry about the money and some of them were worried about my future.

So finally, I went to the school and they were so happy with the delivery of the sessions and the principal told me to please come back again next year. It was a very good session. I was happy and satisfied with the principal's feedback.

I told her that it will not be possible because I am going back to my hometown as I had no money left with me. She felt sad for me.

I thanked her for the opportunity and left for the paying guest.

In all these days, I had tried to convince so many philanthropists, met new people, tried to build social connections so that I could take my idea to the maximum schools. But I failed miserably. I had no money left with me and also, I lost the hope for the finances.

I told my mother that I am going tomorrow to my hometown. She was sad and also worried about me. She told me to send her the famous silk saree of Banaras now Varanasi. It gave me so much pleasure. I thanked her for everything. The love she showered on me all these days. To allow me to stay with her paying guest when I had no money to give it to her. She fed me food with love. The bond we shared was so divine that I wanted to fulfil her wish immediately but I had no money left. Whatever the small money I had left was for the journey ahead to my hometown.

After spending ten years studying and working for various companies I finally came back to my hometown. The expression of the family was mixed. Some were acting happy and some were acting unhappy. Mother, the aunt and the younger brother were there to support my cause. But my father was very-very upset with my decision. He had already left hope in me. His pride had been broken. I am his pride but when I took the decision which put him against me it was so hard for him to manage with me under the same roof.

It was completely my fault. I wanted to make him proud. I wanted to assure him that one day you will be proud of me. But the time did not work according to the sanctity of the emotions. It becomes harder with the sanctity of the emotions.

This is the irony of the time.

My father and I were definitely not on good terms with each other as I was also frustrated with the failure of my project. I failed to get the publisher for my first book. That was the only hope for me to gain money. I had to also work along with my father in our grocery store. My father had built this business from scratch. He was very good at his business. He had also failed several times before running this business successfully.

He had one great specialty. He was a great social worker. I actually realized his stature when I started working with him. People of all ages in the society bow in front of him. Not because of any fear but with the respect he had gained through the welfare of the needy. Everyone respects me because they knew me as his son. They called me and praised me about my father's character and the work he had done in the society, for the society. Once one rich merchant had told me, I cannot trust anyone with my money except your father. This kind of personality he was carrying in the society. Everyone respects him from the very bottom of their heart.

But I had in my anger disrespected him many times. Not intentionally but because of the situations that had been created by the time. I was so immature to understand his pain that he had lost his pride. He always told others with pride that his son is an aircraft mechanic.

But what went on with him when I broke his pride? What went on with him when I broke my promise to make him proud?

It was a very tough situation for me and for him to manage all these emotions, to balance all these emotions, to turn the tables.

It was a very tough situation for me because the mission which I was on demands consistency, dedication, hard work and knowledge.

"Knowledge is the tool which we most of the time underestimate.

There is a difference between information and knowledge.

Knowledge is the key which opens the layer of the mind and helps you to reach at its depth and explore the unconscious of your own mind.

On the other hand, information is like a hammer of the goldsmith which he uses to shape the metal. He keeps striking the hammer on the metal which is our memory to bring it into a particular shape required for the time being.

We use information most of the time when we are giving some exams. Because most of us had experienced that what we had learned in our school and colleges will forget with time.

This is the major difference with the information and knowledge. Information never remains with you and on the other hand, Knowledge always stays with you.

Information gives you the idea about the product. But if you want to gain the insights of how things work then you have to work on gaining knowledge which means to learn to explore your potential. In this way you can unite with nature from where every idea springs out.

The only quest you have is to find out your own potential.

Why is it important?

Because we all are made up of nature. Nature is the major element which constitutes every being on this planet, being it a human, insects, trees, animals, bacteria, other organisms etc.

The beautiful thing of nature has given us all some speciality. Like, a wood to become a matchstick, a paper, a tree to give oxygen and a land to grow the crop and to hide in its depth the oil and so many other qualities etc.

The same way a human being has been designated with so many specialties which he has to discover in this quest called life. That's the reason which gives meaning to our life.

Otherwise, why has this play been created?"

I had to find out the students in my hometown because this is really important for me that I should consistently work on my mission. Therefore, I started again visiting the schools in my hometown with the same intensity as before.

I had to reach more and more students. I soon got more than two schools to volunteer there. I had completed my sessions successfully in all the schools.

But this process was really tiring for me. Because I had to visit so many schools and convince them about the idea on which most of them showed no interest.

I felt like something was going wrong. Then once a famous college in my hometown had called me to teach there for three months because their philosophy lecturer had been hospitalized for some reason.

At first this opportunity made me happy but there was a tint of fear as I had never studied academic philosophy before. How would I teach the students?

But I was confident that I could handle it. So, I took up the opportunity. That opportunity has given me the platform to explore your potential. I took full advantage of that opportunity. The students started liking my teaching and they started enjoying my lectures. I also felt so much attachment with that place with the time.

This duty of mine was giving me so much pleasure, freedom and satisfaction at the psychological level.

That day I realized that at a psychological level every human being had only one need and that is to realize their potential.

We always focused on fulfilling our physical needs, be it food, shelter, money, sex, clothes. But what about the psychological need?

Parents and society and most of us are looking at the wrong side for happiness by fulfilling our physical needs. But what about the psychological needs? Real happiness drives from satisfaction at the psychological level.

How would they know that?

Students really made me proud when after three months they told me that their results were out and they all had passed in the subject.

College gave me more lectures and told me to continue for the next session. I was loaded with the lectures. I enjoyed being a lecturer. It gave me so much happiness to be there and teach those students. I actually felt united with the internal power in those moments and the wisdom was just flowing out like the radio waves were carrying the frequency of hidden energy in those words and connecting them at the psychological level with the source of the knowledge in them.

It was such a beautiful experience and I was filled with gratitude for all the love showered on me by my mentor, Shiva. In all these times, he was with me in the form of wisdom, satisfaction, challenges, failures, hope, patience, love, respect.

The only thing which made me anxious those days was the pain of my father. I was unable to make them understand the sanctity of the idea. But I was sure that one day he would be proud of me.

I was not spending much time at my grocery store. I spent only two to three hours at the store. I had my duty toward my father too and therefore, I always ate after he ate the food. I opened the store and cleaned it and then I went to the college and then after the college, I came back to the store and the father went for lunch and thereafter, me and my mother had our lunch.

This was our daily routine which we followed till the date. He was the supreme for me. I had to do my duties but also, I had to take care of his comforts.

Soon the year had passed which was full of the struggle with the father but it was also good for me as it had given

me so much of the beautiful memories and so much of the
learning.

5

Determination

New year had arrived with all its splendor. People were passing wishes to each other. But at the core of everybody everything was the same perhaps. Some were satisfied with what they had and some were pushing themselves for the success of their idea. Some may have set their new goals. Some were making new resolutions. Some were preparing for the exams. For some everything was the same as last year.

My father is on good terms now. Something had changed with the time. Perhaps he had accepted the situation. Perhaps he had accepted my fate. He really wanted me to be an aircraft mechanic and stay there in the job. He knew that business was tough and therefore, I should keep working. Small towns had not much scope and there was nothing much to do, he said. Maybe he was right.

But I was determined and I had full faith in my idea. I knew that if I had given this potential there would definitely be a chance of its success.

"In this world, everything has some meaning. There is nothing in this world which is without meaning. So, I had to keep my head down and keep pushing myself."

I had no idea what challenges and failures were there in the future waiting for me. And I never think of the future. I always stayed busy in the moment which had so many lessons for me to learn and share.

Exams were on the edge and we all were very busy with our lectures. We as a team are working out the best to bring the best results.

Soon the admissions had opened for the next session. Results had come of my class and they all had passed the examination.

We all were busy with the admissions and I was so happy with the results.

Soon the news broke out all over the media that we all had to close the entire shops in the market and schools and colleges as some virus had been spread out of the sudden until further order from the government.

I immediately took the permission from the principal and ran toward my store. Father was busy packing the stuff and police were all around imposing government orders on the merchants and the common public wandering here and there and moving from one place to another. In a fraction of the time the whole market went silent and people were in hurry toward their homes. Within no time everything became quiet.

Everyone was talking about the virus. Social media and all the news channels running the same news over and over again.

No one knows exactly what was going on. Some people were happy and some people were sad. Some were enjoying it as a holiday and some were crying, shouting because they lost the only source of their income. Some had to leave their workplace and some had to arrange the food for their family.

Doctors, scientists and the government of the country were dealing with the emergency of the situation. They were working on manufacturing the anti-virus. They had the huge challenge of the time. They had less time and they had to give out the results to the people of the country. All the citizens of the country had only hoped left i.e. our doctors and their team working in the hospitals, clinics, camps and whatever the demand of the situation and time.

Our government and the whole team of the medical department of the country had managed the situation so well and arranged free medicine camps to all their citizens of their country as doctors and scientists of the country were working day and night and finally they had manufactured the first indigenous anti-virus dose COVAVAXIN.

When some of the media channels challenged the efforts of the doctors and their own government and degraded their research, COVAVAXIN was the befitting answer to them.

That day Indians recognized their potential.

On the other hand, common people and the groups and the NGO's all came together to help their needy citizens and provide them food and shelter of the need of the hour.

We Indians had left no stone unturned as a doctor, government and the common citizen to help each other in that difficult period in the history of the world.

Government had allowed for a few hours to the merchants in the town and the cities to open their grocery store so that everyone had their necessities fulfilled.

Me and the father now get the pass to open our grocery store. We were allowed some time to open our grocery store. We were now back on our duty after three days of the sudden situation raised out of China as we all got to know.

I had messaged all my friends regarding the opening of the store and they all had visited me and bought the groceries and helped me and my family in that difficult situation at the time.

Now my father and I are working together. He now started believing in my skills in running the store. He was happy with my efforts to bring customers. He was now taking more interest in his work which he had suddenly lost in the last year because of my decisions related to my career.

My mission was put on hold by the emergency of the situation and I did not have any idea what I should do now?

Months had passed and I went busy in the grocery store. I left the job in the college too because there were very few students left in the college and new admissions were so few and no students were interested in pursuing a career in philosophy. Therefore, the college had removed the subject from its curriculum.

College was going through a very tough time. Because most of the parents of the students were doing labor and they had not enough money left to maintain their child studies because of the pandemic.

College had not enough students left and therefore, no money to pay their teachers. Things were getting worse with time.

For some of us maybe that time was not that much hard but for some it was so hard to manage the food and their children's studies.

Lots of businesses had been affected and so many had lost their jobs. It was a very tough time. I too had lost my mission which I had started with so much passion.

It was like a mission had been lost in time. The mission never happened. l was reading books. I had engaged myself in learning all those days. But I lost direction. Schools went online. I had no idea how I would reach the students? They and their parents were also dealing with the new online scenario.

Schools had no time for any extracurricular activity. Our grocery store also needed some refurbishment and changes. So, I spent so much time changing the entire layout of the store. To protect the grains from the rats in the store is the major task I was dealing with. Inflation made the small businesses fall and customers started moving toward the big stores.

I assumed that was the end of my mission and with that the end of my idea. I was so much attached with the college but what to do as I had no choice but to wait. Keep patience and keep alive in my heart the hope for what I had started is the only remedy. The reason why I had started it was that it seemed to have lost its meaning.

I had to keep patience. That was the only thing which gave me happiness and now I was distanced from that too. Working in my grocery store gave me happiness but that idea made me alive. It gave me meaning. It gave me freedom. It gave meaning to everything actually. Why is it important for me? Why did I start it? What is its role in others' lives? How can it create an impact in others' lives? Everything.

Shall I let it go? Was this the end of this journey?

I had to keep the hope alive. Maybe I had to find a new way of reaching the students. Shall I start the online classes? Can I do that? I had never tried that before?

Do not lose hope, I told myself. I had to try new ways. I had to work on some new ideas. So, I had started gaining more knowledge. I had to create something new which motivates me and which will energize me.

After six months of studying I had created a new idea and started again with the same passion as before and started visiting the schools. I had visited so many schools. I tried to visit so many schools in the major cities of my district. But this time, no school had shown any interest in it. I had tried to partner with the training institutes. That too had failed.

Finally, after wandering for one month one institute had shown interest in it and they told me to carry out your program into our institute. I was so happy and I told my mother about the same. She expressed gratitude.

I went to the institute and met the staff and they told me to introduce myself to your class. I went to the class and the response was good. The next day no one showed up except two students and the manager told me that students were not interested in these kinds of classes. If you want any help let me know.

He was such a gentleman. But the major challenge now for me is to attract students to the institute. I called them many times in the following months but no students had enrolled, they said.

I was tired of the failures. Schools were not interested. Students were not interested. How do I convince them?

Something was definitely lacking. Ten months of hard work with no result and I did not understand the cause.

Maybe determination works like this. It tests the patience of the diligent. My faith in my idea demands patience.

I had started writing a manuscript and finished it in the following six months. Now I have to publish it. So, I had sent sample copies of the manuscript to so many publishers. After a month, I got rejection mail from most of the publishers and few of them had not replied as they had their policy "you will hear from us in four to twelve weeks if not then take it as rejection".

It was such a tiring process. Keep trying and then you fail. Every effort brought the same result. FAIL.

I was so tired. Need a break.

I am desperately looking for a girl who will rescue me from all these struggles for some time being.

Don't know where she is?

6
Visualization

Failure and success, they are not the two shores of the journey.

Really?

I did not expect this after so much of the failures and working so hard till now on my idea, I told Shiva.

We have to understand the journey is not about the success and the failure. We need to be profound and look into the other aspects of this journey.

What do you mean?

Every idea is born with the seed of the attachment. This attachment will push you toward the results. It will make you think of the consequences. It will create the imaginations and the dreams. Dreams which definite the results gave birth to hope and strengthened the faith of the determined. The dreamer works day and night and tries everything to achieve that dream of him.

There is the thin line which we have to be taken care of. You have to control the idea rather than the idea controls you.

Attachment will create the pair of opposites: success and failure.

We all have to find the balance in between them. Imbalance was the main cause that made us anxious. We want to be successful at any cost. We do not want to fail. What if we failed? All that thoughts arise out of the attachment and there we trap our-self into the play of the illusion.

Balance we need to maintain at the psychological level. It means to know your state of mind.

It is very-very common that most people never look at the states of the mind. We have to understand that whatever the situation we will create in our mind that will create our outer circumstances.

Right now, when you are looking at the situation as a failure, the main reason is that you have not understood the meaning of your purpose. You had confined the purpose into two shores, success and failure.

Learn to look at the situation first at the psychological level. Learn to look within first. What is your state of mind?

As you had said, I was tired. That means there is a cause of this tiredness and what is that cause?

My failed attempt, said I.

Absolutely. You have to understand that you have to free yourself from this cause.

Unless you have not freed yourself from this cause, you will remain the victim.

What should I do?

Let it go, said Shiva. Enjoy the journey. I told you, do not limit your life to this mission. Mission has been given to you to become responsible, to grow internally, to explore the different aspects of life, to enjoy the vastness of the journey, to actualize yourself and most importantly to find the balance at the psychological level.

Do not attach with it. Free yourself. Free yourself from the cause. As you are not the doer.

Then who is the doer? I asked Shiva.

Shiva smiled and said, listen to this creation of the being.

Everything is composed of two these elements jeev and prakarti (male and female) in this universe. Understand jeev as the seed and nature (prakarti) as the womb.

Nature consists of eight elements: mind, ego, logic, air, water, earth, fire and ether.

These eight elements when composed with jeev, creates every being in this universe: living and nonliving.

Everything is composed out of these two main elements.

Nature is very vast and it flows simultaneously and it continually expands.

Nature plays all the roles in being. Jeev had only one role to give the being its purpose but nature is the real teacher. Nature creates the thoughts, the reasons, the color, the voice, the personality of the being, the illusion.

How do you look, what is your race, what is your color and what do you think about yourself: weak or strong, black and white, rich or poor? All that is because of the workings of nature.

What makes each of us different is our appearance and our roles and that is made up of the very nature and jeev. No one can control it. There are infinite possibilities in this creation. It can create anything with these two elements we can't even imagine.

Whatever it creates, it creates through the idea, the desire. It puts the desire into the depth of the mind of the being and all the nature which is in us feeds that desire to grow as a mother feeds the infant in her womb.

Now the purpose which comes from the jeev is the specialty of the being. We have to discover that specialty which means to self-actualize and realize your potential. Once you realize your potential you can start using that potential through the means of learning.

Learning feeds nature and nature feeds the idea which drives the action and then our actions change that idea into reality.

But this process does not only mean to stress yourself, to put all your energy only to make your idea the reality. This process does not only mean to self-actualize.

This process wants us to learn to balance your energy. To balance your thoughts. To explore the psychological space and visit the unconscious and take a look into it. You will find that there are so many beliefs which we had created in our childhood. It was created by the actions and the teachings of the parents, teachers, our friendships, our society and by our education system.

There are so many people involved in shaping us. It depends on our environment what we will become as a person? What will be our worth?

But worth does not only depend on the subjective success of our idea. As there are so many beliefs which are shaping us in our day to day life we have to understand them too. Therefore, development is not dependent on the success of the idea but it is a continuous process of learning our-self so that we can reach the source of the creation which resides within us. It is a lifelong process.

You can understand it to discover the truth which resides within us. As I told you before there are only two elements: jeev and prakarti. But these elements came from the truth which cannot be defined. No explanation can be sufficient to make you understand what is truth? How does it look? But in one way you can understand it and that you can realize it is in the form.

Everything has a form. Love has the form of the girl. Fear has the form of a dog. Comfort has the form of a home. Wisdom has the form of a teacher. jeev and prakarti have the form of parents, and truth is the form of you.

So, this journey has been made to discover yourself as the truth.

Therefore, do not get stuck in the pair of opposites: success and failure. Know yourself. Go deep into the unconscious of your mind and discover the truth that is residing there behind the mayhem of the emotions in silence.

Learn everything in this journey as you have learned your goal. There are infinite possibilities of learning. You should not confine it to your goal. But make your goal the center of your learning.

The alarm rang and I woke up.

I got the idea what Shiva wanted me to understand:

1. To free from attachment
2. To find the balance
3. To free from the cause

Do not confine your life between the two shores: from where we all had started and to the final point. Some may reach the final point as there is not any final point except the truth but some were not.

What had they found there? Have you ever asked them? They did not actually find what they thought they would find there. Wonder! That means life wants us to explore the other aspects of life itself.

Our life is the product of our thoughts. So, it is our responsibility to work on our thoughts and try to understand the causes which are present in the unconscious mind, which is important to find balance in life.

I had to create the union with the truth within. That may help me find peace in the current situation.

I needed love, I needed art at that moment of the time which I was desperately looking for in the form of the girl and the poetry.

7
A poetry

After the long wait of eleven years finally I met a girl who had filled my heart with the song.

A song which made me a poet.

I did not understand how to approach her as I knew her from my childhood so it made me a little uncomfortable. But my heart was beating very fast and loud. I did not understand what had happened to my heart all of the sudden. Just a minute before everything was normal and when she came it started beating loudly. I had to place my hand on my chest and verbally spoke to it to calm down.

First, I ignored the indication which was given to me by my heart. But then I gave it a second thought to give it a try. If there is any truth let me discover it.

I approached her and asked her about her whereabouts. She told me that she was living out of the country as she got a new job a few months back and came home for a few weeks. I was happy but sad too as she was working abroad now and I wanted to live with my parents and to handle my grocery store and work out something new out of my idea.

I congratulate her for her new job. I asked her about her last job. She told that it was her financial conditions that push her to leave that job and settled abroad. I told her that I needed her help to build connections in the school where she was teaching before moving abroad and she gave me her contact number to talk further on that issue.

I was surprised and happy with her frankness. Now I had her number so I could talk to her at any time.

I was now at peace for at least I had her number. I had to be patient with my words. It had to be meaningful communication rather than unnecessary talks.

I had to find a way to tell her about my feelings!

"Everything has started like this in our life which really made us so impatient and then slowly it took over our mind and attached us with that particular idea and then we become the energy of which the effect has to be passed on to the other person and the world as the story weaved and unfold so many emotions and left their impact and their consequences."

I was overwhelmed by the emotion of love and this time I will not let her go, I told to myself.

Love which was not in our control and it never will be in anyone's control entered on their own into our life and then entangled us and made us express it in the form of art, being it the poetry, music, dance, painting and so on.

The emotions I was going through had never experienced before. It was so pure, so powerful and so enigmatic that I had to use poetry to express them and I had started writing that page by page and it became a notebook.

The purity of the love which had shown to me in those poetic words was impossible to understand by the other side unless it will not be touched by the love.

So, what do I do?

I was so entangled in that moment of love and didn't find out the way to come out of that powerful yet enigmatic form of love.

It had the power at the same time to free you from all the bad thoughts and the bad habits. It was so beautiful to experience that relief that liberated you suddenly and made you realize the meaning of freedom and to be in the vicinity of the truth.

Love for sure frees you from all the unnecessary thoughts which takes you away from the truth.

But Love has one condition which I did not yet know.

I was walking and walking and continuously imagining her and writing my poetry. I wanted that poetry to share with her. So, I decided to tell her what I felt about her.

One day, I messaged her about the feeling which I had for her. Her reaction was like I had thrown a bomb on her and she blocked me immediately!

"I knew, there were so many and so many who had experienced the same.

My sympathy with you all!

Its hard to guess why? Don't know why girls do this? "

And I had messaged her through another means and asked her to unblock me as I was sorry for my words.

She after a delay of one day unblocked me as I have messaged her many times in a day. She had saved my poetry to go to waste!

Love was blossoming I thought as she had unblocked me. This false notion was the beautiful thing at that moment. It motivates me to write more, to try again and fail again.

That false notion was the only hope which I had at that time being which I wanted to be true.

Now, I started with little hesitation. I was trying my best to not hurt her again with my words so I was not sending her any caring messages as she was unpredictable at that moment.

Love was struggling and I could not do anything but wait for the right moment. Days had passed by the good morning and good night messages. As she was only messaged back when I messaged her and sometimes not.

Gradually, I started with other messages about her day to day routine and how she manages the food chores while doing job?

Definitely she replied and then more and more messages and then one day I started sharing with her my poetry and told her that she was the inspiration behind that.

I wanted to tell her my feelings which were not fiction but came out of the unconscious of the heart which has its own way to express their work.

I asked her about her liking of the poetries. She said she had no interest in the poetries but she liked them. I liked her reply and the false notions were definitely in the sky as she knew that she was the inspiration behind those poetries.

But Love plays its own role in the mind at both ends. I do not know how it works? But one thing was sure that I was entangled.

You have to go through dual consequences: entangled and freedom. Love was hard to play but what could anyone do if love wants to play?

What was she thinking?

I had not the slightest clue other than my false notions. I was telling her my emotions in the form of poetries but I didn't have any idea how those poetries affected her state of mind.

"The cause and the effect are the essence of our very actions."

As I was in love and that was the cause which springs out in me on their own toward her and its effect was the expressions of the poetries. But what was on the mind on the other end? Did these poems create any effect there?

I had no idea. It was impossible to know the mind of the girl on the other end.

Love travels between the two ends: one was my mind and the others were her. But why wasn't anything blooming at the other end?

Finally, after three months of all those love games I asked her to marry me and she told me no. I can't do it.

I asked her why?

She said I had no feelings for you.

That made me upset. I was like nothing in this world had happened without meaning. If this love had blossomed on their own for you then definitely it has some cause!

I wanted to know the cause. Otherwise what was the purpose of all those poetries and all those emotions, those moments? Those moments were the period of prayer for me. It was so pure, so artistic in their expression which I had by no means could experience them without her present at the other end.

And why only she? Why not anyone else?

Those questions were running through my mind as I was trying to find out the cause of that situation.

"I have to let her go", a voice came from within. It was impossible for me to believe what that voice was demanding.

How will I let her go?

The girl about whom I had thought day and night, how can I let her go?

This is the irony with love. "If you want to catch it will run away and if you let her go it will stay with you", voice said.

How absurd is this the rule of love?

But this is what the moment was demanding of me and the rule of love too. I have to let her go.

I deleted her number and let her go. But it was not that much easy. I stayed attached to that cause and only by deleting her number I was only doing half of the job. I had to detach myself from her mentally. I had to come out of the effect of that cause which sprouted there in the unconscious because of her.

Detachment!

I had to learn this process. Otherwise I would go through the negative effects of the cause too.

Everything has happened to teach you this detachment! That was the only answer I got from that meeting with her.

And that's the reason for that cause of the love too. To make you understand the importance of detachment.

"This world has not guaranteed you what it shows you. It is actually meaning something else. It has hidden so much more in the form of learning.

That's why you have to learn to let go. That is the time to detach yourself from within. Because outer actions without initiating inner actions will not bring results."

I was in a bad state. I did not want to lose again. But this journey was more than success and failure, so I had to come out of this and start with the new thing which would bring me back on the track. The track which I had lost for some time now.

Six months had passed into all this. I had to come out of this and started working again on the idea which I started after meeting Shiva.

Now after six months everything was normal. I was busy with my idea but there was a wanting so deep. It felt like a deep driving desire. Nothing felt stronger than that wanting to me. I don't know why? I was waiting for her silently. I was afraid of the matrimony and all other proposals which was coming for marriage at that time. I wanted to stay close to her and therefore, prayed to bring her back anyhow into the life.

Then one day she suddenly came up unexpectedly. I messaged her and she replied but not immediately but as you know after a lot of hours. No, not hours! but days! I felt so happy because she was the only subject matter to me more than anthing and that was true.

At that moment I realised love which I had never understood before. I had written "lyrical fragments" which realised me the truth of everything. There was nothing more beautiful than these lines which I had understood.

<u>Lyrical fragments:</u>

1. You are my most beautiful prayer!
2. You are the whole cosmos manifested in a form! You are such a divine!
3. The time I opened my eyes, world presents itself and created an illusion that you and me are separate and far away. I understood it now this world is a lie.
4. your impression is still fresh in my memory like a spring comes forth out of love in a winter and gave its embracers a feeling of joy which lasts for a little while and left the impression of eternal union.
5. This is not something that I can buy from this world. You, definitely bring with you some soma, which belongs to the other world; which has left an impression of an eternal touch, which I have never tasted before. I believe this is ssame as effloresecence, flower in its bloom, born out its colour, which made it more beautiful for the viewer who left it untouched and fresh.

6. What left in me is you! And that made me more beautiful than before and that is what I want to protect. This is the only reason I want to stay alone, as you are the most precious jewel which i have found in these momentary years which successfully deviated me with their illusions but at last you come again and protected me!

7. Now that I understood, you my love, are a fanatsy came out of my imagination which was before abstract in my unconscious. But how can it be so! I have met you here in this physical momentary world. How can this be so that you are my fantasy! Yet if you are! than I want to live with that.

8. I want to, I have to protect myself from this momentary world because it is deviating me, creating space between you and me.

9. I felt myself beautiful as I found you within. Is there anything which can made me beautiful without? Does it not true that the appearances are momentary? They are temporary! But you are eternal my love! Will always remain same as you are now. That is your unfathomable beauty!

10. This world is a lie. I do not believe in it anymore. You too should not believe in it. You are still deviated by these illusions. Otherwise you have recognised me, my love!

11. I have waited so many years before meeting you. Deviated by so many faces but finally I found my house where I can rest amd sleep. No more deviation, my love!

12. Now everything has done. I don't think there is anything left for me in this world. My purpose has fulfilled as I have found you!

13. We can meet here in this dark silent place, where no one can see us and therefore, can separate us. Here are no illusions like a physical world. Here we can meet

anytime, whenever we want without any interruptions and fear.

14. Never have I ever will learnt the true nature of this momentary world if I have never met you. Everytime this world creates deviations which made me restless but now, as I have you my love! Now I am at rest! The reality of this world has unveiled. You, yet do not recognised me but its not your fault. This world is illusionary and that its true nature. Its nature is to create illusions so that one cannot reach its shore. ButI, who recognised you, am grateful to you. This place is definitely illusionary but also this place is the place of union where I met you!

15. Sex is the very cheap and small term people used for the union. Union is not always physical. It is momenatry too, as ours! It gace birth to an art and so to an artist! I am grateful to you for such a union! which is impossible without you. It is definitely momentary but it too has the lasting impression. Who knows that I became so rich to have you? I have never ever experience such richness before! You bring life or should I say, you gave birth in me to an art and treasure!

16. I have completely disconnected from the outer world that is the power of your presence in my life! All day seems like a prayer to me! I am just picturing you into my mind's eye and it puts me into ecstasy.

17. What I want is the lasting impression! It is the same phenomenon like a reflection of a passerby on the glass of a door in a daylight where he can see himself as he is standing in front of it. I am the passerby and you are the glass. I have just saw my reflection in you.

18. I do not want your love! What I want is that one day you will realise that no one can love you as I do!

19. Everyone is a passerby! They all will left their impression on your mind which lasts depend on your intimacy.

20. She is a superior and yet at the same time dowm to earth woman. Whenever I have looked at her I felt like I am looking at the absolute beauty which is eternal and cannot modify. But whenever she adorned herself, gave a touch of change to her appearance, it felt she was the only one who could modify the absolute beauty. No one can but only she can just by covering her head with a cotton scarf.

So many poetries (urdu) I had written at that time period. I am sharing here just two of them:

1. *"Teri hasraton ka qaafila guzar jayega, Dil mein jo bhi hai dil mein hi reh jayega.*

Qismat ka lekhaa-jokhaa jaldi khul jayega, tu nahi to koi aur hi apni qismat mein ayega.

Khuda bhi hamari vafaa ik din duniya ko dikhaega, Qalam ka zor ik din apni jarur chaegaa.

Aaftaab shab-e-Gam ko ik roz mita jayega, Ye banda ik din "Ashish" sab ko nazar ayega.

Tu nahi to koi aur is dil ki aag ko jagayega, Ye dard nahi vo jo jaate-jaate jayega. "

Meaning-

Hasrat- Desire, qaafila- Tribe,

lekhaa-jokhaa- Calculation, Vafaa- Loyalty, Qalam- Pen,

Aaftaab- The sun, Shab-e-Gam- Night of sorrow.

2. *Humne jo dekha to ye dekha ki , jisne bhi use dekha raah-e-fraar na seekha.*

jisko bhi usne bulaya , hasaya, paas bithaya, usne fir kabhi raah-e-shar'a na seekha.

bhuton ne pdaa hai bhut kuch, lekin khud ko padna kisi ne na seekha.

unki qayamat aankhon mein dekhna hai, humne ki kisne marna na seekha.

kitni kitaabein, kitne rahbar, kitne phalsafe, jo unke dar par gya usne fir vo seekha jo kahin na seekha.

unki nigah-e-mast mein jisne bhi dekha, fir usne chalna na seekha.

mast-e-raah mein justjuu ki e "Ashish", raah-e-talab bhi gai aur koi hunar bhi na seekha.

Meaning:

raah-e-fraar - way to escape, raah-e-shar'a - religious rituals

rahbar - Teacher, nigah-e-mast - intoxicated eyes

mast-e-raah - drunk, justjuu - quest

raah-e-talab - the path of desire

So this is what I had been gone through all those years. What love had done to me! I am now lost my appetite for everything.

8
New Beginning

We all are so tempted when we will look into the future and imagine how our future should look like.

That temptation pushes you to work hard or just sit and wait for somebody to come and give you everything whatever you had imagined then in the time.

I had to come out of that dream and started working hard on the idea which I had started once seven years ago and left everything for that.

I really need to come out of that situation and bring my life back on track and unite with the self by the power of the idea and its ways of working.

I had to find a new approach to use this idea. I had to create something new again which is impressive and really worked out.

I had to start reading books again and what I had bought by chance was Ignited minds by APJ Abdul Kalam.

I had started reading with the hope that I had to come to the current situation of my mind. As I had completed the book I got the idea of what I needed to do with the idea? How I had to present it to the students?

Now was the time to implement that idea and I had started implanting that idea in my life and what I had experienced was that the idea had started showing me the laws which were a very useful part of my daily life.

I practiced them daily for one to one and half hours and it helped me not only to come out of the situation but also gave me a deep understanding about the laws of success and also hidden the motivation which consistently uses that power which resides in that idea and creates the effect into the being.

If those laws were affecting me and then it definitely affects others too and that made me sure about those laws.

That idea worked so well for me that I not only came out of the entangled ness of love but also understood the lesson of letting go and how to stay motivated when you had nothing but the hope that something was going to change soon. That idea continuously builds belief within.

Mesmerized by the working of the laws I decided to open a digital classroom in the town where any needy child can study for free of cost on the computers or the laptops from the best teachers around the world and give his life a meaning. Therefore, I started my own counseling center where I will guide them and help them to understand the significance of education in our life. How can we change our life with the proper use of education? As I had never ever realized that I came so close to the reality which I had never imagined before to run the center as a counselor. In this process, I met some good people from my hometown which assures me that they will help me in building the digital classroom.

That identity which I had just realized was so harmonious that it had unfolded the layers within the depth of the unconscious which had shown me not only the laws but the subtlety of the universe which I found not anywhere but within.

As I gained clarity I also had to liberate partially from the web of the illusion which was always there which was always working in the background as our beliefs kneaded with the ingredients of ego, greed, lust, selfishness, hate, pleasure and so on.

Illusion is the subtlest element which we all are run by and the only savior is the wisdom which came to our life in the form of the teacher and the love.

To realize that every thought which you carry and put into this world has been filled with so much illusion. No one can free themselves from the touch of illusion and that is the main player which maintains the silence in the wise man.

When the wise understand that most of the thoughts sprout out of illusion then he learned the art of silence. He knew that the major element working there was the ego, lust and desires. They are the main component of illusion and to handle them wisely was not even easy for the wisest.

This whole web of thoughts and ideologies has been weaved by these elements which has pushed us toward the different journeys and has created different perspectives and made the play beautiful and filled with so much of diversity.

This illusion is the hero which played with the minds of so many of us and created in reality the one the hero and the other the villain.

It is the illusion which let us go and entangled us. It all depends on it. It is the major force which runs in the depth of the unconscious away from the conscious thoughts of the human being could ever imagine would be the puppet in the hands of this vastness.

Truth which is silently sitting there in the unconscious has looked at everything without the slightest of interference and has unveiled the illusion and watched her play.

It is the truth who has placed there in the midst of all the illusions. But when it will come into action no one knows.

The wise which resides in us is the only shield against illusion and the rescuer of our mind from anxiety, depression and ambitions.

When you look at the wise person you can only look at the surface of how it appears to you but the real thing which is working in him is in the depth of the unconscious of his mind and that is the shield which has changed him and his perspective and his way of lifestyle, his vision about the reality.

What he is seeing is actually the eternal truth which is not easy to understand by the others because of the illusion that runs in our background and therefore, hard to believe and work on it.

So how can we come out of all this?

Why has this play been created?

Who is the author of this play?

Why is he playing that play?

None of the above questions has so much significance in our life as the only single most question that how can we become self-actualized?

When we focus on self-actualization, every philosophy and psychology of your being automatically unfolds in you and expresses itself to you in the form of your potential in this journey of your life.

Therefore, it is the most important step that wherever we are and whatever our backgrounds, if we actually want to know the truth, want to liberate ourselves from the illusion, we have to grow from within and that is only possible when we have a goal in our life and a courage to fulfill it.

Nothing matters more than self-actualization right now in our life.

Self-actualization is the need of every human being at the psychological level. Without self-actualizing yourself you cannot experience happiness wherever you can go or whatever you can buy or how much you can save the money.

You have to understand the essence of this play. This play has been created to play but what happens if you will not play?

You have to find out your role, your character in this play and must have the caliber which will make you a significant player in this play.

When you look around your outer world, open the blindfold and naked the unconscious and look into it. You will find all the power and the potential present in there which you were missing into your outer world.

With this advice, I end my story here and I take your permission.

As I had shared the idea of successfully establishing the venture and the laws of freedom in the form of the title of the chapters and my journey of this book itself. Hope you all will use this idea and live a happy and dignified and independent life.

End Note

Psychology transcends space and time. Whatever was your state of mind ten or fifty or eighty years ago will remain the same throughout the age unless you will not develop the habit of learning.

Psychology works on the learning process. That's the only way to progress at the psychological level.

That's y, we all have to learn to grow internally more than externally. Otherwise there will be no growth if the thousand years have passed for you.

www.ingramcontent.com/pod-product-compliance
Lightning Source LLC
Chambersburg PA
CBHW020508160726
47991CB00007B/2853